The

an

Product

Mark Ravenhill was born in Haywards Heath, West Sussex, in 1966. Literary Manager of Paines Plough between December 1995 and June 1997, he was appointed Artistic Associate at the National Theatre in the summer of 2002. His first full-length play *Shopping and Fucking*, produced by Out of Joint and the Royal Court Theatre, opened at the Royal Court Theatre Upstairs in September 1996 and was followed by a national tour. It transferred to the Queen's Theatre, West End, June 1997, and was followed by an international tour. His other works include *Faust is Dead* (Actors' Touring Company, national tour, 1997); *Sleeping Around*, a joint venture with three other writers (Salisbury Playhouse, February 1998, transferring to the Donmar Warehouse, London, followed by national tour); *Handbag* (Actors' Touring Company, Lyric Hammersmith Studio, 1998, followed by national tour); *Some Explicit Polaroids* (for Out of Joint, Theatre Royal, Bury St Edmunds, transferring to the New Ambassadors, London, October 1999); *Lost and Found* (broadcast BBC2, May 2000); *North Greenwich* (play reading by Paines Plough, 'Wild Lunch' series); *Feed Me* (broadcast BBC Radio 3, November 2000); *Mother Clap's Molly House* (Lyttelton, National Theatre, August 2001, transferring to the Aldwych Theatre, West End, February 2003); *Totally Over You* (performed as part of 'Shell Connections' youth theatre festival, National Theatre, July 2003); *Moscow* (Royal Court International Playwrights' Season, March 2004); *Education* (read as part of 'National Headlines' season of topical verbatim monologues, National Theatre, 2004); and *Citizenship* ('Shell Connections' festival, National Theatre, 2005).

Mark Ravenhill

The Cut

and

Product

B L O O M S B U R Y

LONDON · NEW DELHI · NEW YORK · SYDNEY

Bloomsbury Methuen Drama

An imprint of Bloomsbury Publishing Plc

50 Bedford Square	1385 Broadway
London	New York
WC1B 3DP	NY 10018
UK	USA

www.bloomsbury.com

Bloomsbury is a registered trade mark of Bloomsbury Publishing Plc

First published in the UK in 2006 by Methuen Publishing Limited
Reprinted by Bloomsbury Methuen Drama 2008

British Library Cataloguing-in-Publication Data
A catalogue record for this book is available from the British Library.

ISBN: PB: 978-0-4137-7574-0
ePDF: 978-1-4081-4205-9
ePUB: 978-1-4081-4206-6

Library of Congress Cataloging-in-Publication Data
A catalog record for this book is available from the Library of Congress.

The Cut

Dedicated to the memory of Tim Fraser

The Cut premiered at the Donmar Warehouse, London, on 23 February 2006. The cast was as follows:

Paul	Ian McKellen
John	Jimmy Akingbola
Gita	*
Susan	Deborah Findlay
Mina	*
Stephen	Tom Burke

Director	Michael Grandage
Designer	Paul Wills
Lighting Designer	Paule Constable
Music and Sound Score	Adam Cork

* *Not cast at time of going to press.*

Characters

Scene One	**Paul**
	John
	Gita
Scene Two	**Paul**
	Susan
	Mina
Scene Three	**Paul**
	Stephen

Scene One

A room. A desk. **Paul** *and* **John**.

Paul   Were the searches made?

John   I was searched, yes.

Paul   Was there any unnecessary brutality?

John   No. No, I wouldn't say it was unnecessary brutality.

Paul   Because I need to record any cases of unnecessary . . . I'm compiling a dossier. Which many people are eager to read.

John   I see.

Paul   The last lot were very slack on unnecessary brutality. Blind eyes were turned. You remember?

John   Yes.

Paul   But we intend to be different. We're shining a light on . . . We're coming down, very hard. You see? On unnecessary . . .

John   Yes.

Paul   But we need the figures, so if you were in any way . . .

John   No, no.

Paul   You have to tell me.

John   No.

Paul   Look, to you I know I'm – what? – I'm Authority. Power. Strength. The Father.

John   Well –

Paul   But honestly you must tell me if there was any unnecessary – for the dossier.

John   No.

Paul   You're quite sure?

John   Very sure.

Paul   Well, that's good. Good. Good. No fist?

John   No.

Paul   No boot?

John   No.

Paul   Good. Good. Good.

Beat.

You were searched?

John   Yes.

Paul   Thoroughly?

John   Yes.

Paul   But in such a way as not to . . .

John   Yes, yes, yes.

Paul   Good, good, good. You understand why we have to . . . ?

John   Of course.

Paul   Someone did actually pull a gun on me recently. Little bastard actually got a gun through and pulled it out on me.

John   Shit.

Paul   And fired.

John   Shit.

Paul   I actually saw the bullet coming out of the gun, saw it coming towards me and ducked. Just in time.

John   Shit.

Paul   So as you can imagine I gave those guys out there merry hell. 'Security? Security? Call yourself Security and you let some fucker through with a gun?' We've had to set a new target for performance. Utterly thorough without any unnecessary brutality. Using that performance indicator, how would you say the operatives did? In your experience?

John Well . . .

Paul Excellentverygoodgoodaveragepoor?

John Very good.

Paul So – some room for improvement. But . . . getting there. Good.

He records this in a file.

Now. Can I give you any more information?

John No. I don't think so.

Paul You've read the leaflets?

John I've read everything.

Paul Well . . . good, good. Very . . . impressive.

John I've been preparing for this moment for a long time. Books. The clips. I've thought about this.

Paul Good.

John I wanted to be ready.

Paul Excellent.

John I really wanted to be ready for the Cut.

Paul Yes. Yes. Well, we'll have to see if . . .

John Where are the instruments?

Paul They're with –

John Only in the clips they have the instruments all laid out, you know. On the desk. There. Before I . . . before he . . . walks into the room they're all laid out and then, 'Are you ready for the Cut?' 'Yes.' And – instruments in and –

Paul Pain.

John Pain and then – done.

Paul Yes, well – that was the last lot. All very brutal. All very fast. We're . . . different.

John   Yes?

Paul   Oh yes. We're very different. We've made some changes.

John   Oh. I see.

Paul   We're a force for change. So . . . let's consider some other options.

John   No.

Paul   We're going to look at –

John   No.

Paul   No?

John   I want to . . . I'm here for the Cut. I want the Cut. That's what I'm here for. The Cut.

Paul   And I'm here to look at the options. And as I'm . . . as I'm this side of the desk, we're going to look at the options. We're going to look at your choices. Alright?

John   Alright.

Paul   There's a prison facility. We offer a prison facility to the insane. Are you insane?

John   No.

Paul   Because if you're insane –

John   I'm not insane.

Paul   Although prison doesn't come cheap. You pay. Or – poverty pending – we pay. So nobody's keen on the prison facility. Still, if you're actually insane –

John   I'm not.

Paul   Do you have the paperwork?

John   Here.

He hands **Paul** *a piece of paper.*

Paul   Well, this all seems to be . . . so you're actually sane?

John   Yes.

Paul   Well, that's very impressive. In this day and age. Now, there's the army. Let's think about that.

John   No.

Paul   Or the university. Maybe we should be sending you to the university.

John   No, no. I don't want –

Paul   The army and the university. Much more cost-efficient than prison. Let's talk about –

John   No, no, let's not. Let's not mess about.

Paul   Mess about?

John   Mess about. This, this, this . . . you're the man who does the Cut, right?

Paul   I'm in the office of the building where the Cut is –

John   Then do the Cut. Do the Cut on me.

Paul   This is the office. This is the building. But that doesn't have to define . . . me. You. We have choices. You and me. We can be . . . there's the army, the university, the prison. So much choice.

John   No, no.

Paul   Oh, oh, would you rather be under the last lot?

John   No, no, no.

Paul   Because if you're telling me you'd rather be under the last lot then that, my son, is a political statement, and if you're making political statements, if you're standing here in a public place – and yes, this is classified as a public place – standing in a public space and making political statements then it's the university for you. I'll send you straight off to the university and they'll soon put a stop to these political statements.

John   No, no, no. I wasn't . . . there wasn't anything political, just . . .

Paul   Yes?

John   . . . just I've got this far, you know?

Paul   Of course.

John   Always another office, always another interview, another search, another form to fill. From my village to the town to the city, and now . . . now that I've got this far, I thought you'd just . . . just . . .

Paul   Yes?

John   I thought you were a rubber stamp.

Paul   I am more, I am much much much more than a rubber as you put it stamp.

John   Of course.

Paul   Would I have all this space, all this facility, all this . . . fucking impressive . . . How do I look to you . . . ?

John   Well, yes, impressive.

Paul   And?

John   And, and . . .

Paul   And?

John   Old. As in wise. As in responsible. As in, as in, as in, as in . . .

Paul   Authority.

John   Authoritative.

Paul   As in authoritative authority. Yes. As in burdened with, the burden of . . .

John   Exactly.

Paul   Do you think I tell my wife what I do here? (I have a wife.) Do you think my children . . . ? (One's in prison – expensive – one's in university – cheaper.) Do you think I tell my children what I do here? Have you thought about that?

John   Well, maybe you should. Maybe you should. Maybe. Because, listen, the Cut, I think it's . . . I want the Cut. I think the Cut's a very beautiful . . . a very old and beautiful . . . it's a ritual, a custom, something we . . .

Paul   I don't think so.

John   To actually leave your body.

Paul   Have you any idea of the suffering? The pain? The great screams as the instruments go in?

John   Of course.

Paul   They claw at me. They howl at the sky. It's barbaric.

John   I know all that. All the clips. But I want –

Paul   And I have to carry all this on. Disgusting. You know we actually – off the record – have a working party looking at, considering ending the whole thing.

John   No.

Paul   Off the record.

John   Why?

Paul   Progress. Humanity. Etcetera. Our core values.

John   But that's centuries of . . . you can't wipe out centuries of . . . my grandmother, my uncles, so many centuries –

Paul   You can't stand in the way of core values. None of us can.

John   Everybody had the Cut.

Paul   And for now of course we're carrying it through.

John   Good.

Paul   Just . . . softening the blow. Talking. We get to know you. You get to know us.

John   How does that . . . ?

Paul   For the records.

John   Please. I'd like to see the instruments. I don't want to talk.

Paul   I'll be the judge –

John   This isn't right. This isn't how it's supposed to be. I'm not supposed to get to know you. You're not supposed to talk to me. You're just supposed to show me the instruments.

Paul   New procedures.

John   I haven't heard about –

Paul   There's new procedures all the time. Every day practically. Only this morning I received a directive.

John   Where do you keep the instruments?

Paul   New guidelines for talking. Keep things inclusive.

John   I don't want to talk.

Paul   If you want to see the directive –

John   I'm not going to talk.

Paul   Box files full of the things. Aims. Objectives. Targets. Outcomes. Let me show them. We're very open. It's a root and branch thing.

John   No, no, no. Just – Cut me. Come on. Do it. Do it. Show me the instruments. Get the instruments and Cut me.

Paul   Just – like that – cruel, cold, hard, impersonal?

John   Yes, yes, yes.

Paul   That would make me very unhappy. You'd be in great pain –

John   I know that.

Paul   But also I'd be in great pain. Inside. Enormous pain – physical for you, spiritual for me.

John   Yes. Please. Come on. It's what I want. Fuck's sake – that's what I want.

Paul Are you sure you're not insane?

John You've seen the −

Paul And I suppose we'll have to take their word, but still I've never seen anybody so . . . keen.

John Yes, well . . .

Paul So keen for the Cut. Why are you − ?

John I don't want to talk.

Paul Just a little longer.

John I'd rather we just −

Paul Tell me. Tell me and I'll show you the instruments.

John You've got them?

Paul Of course I've got them. Couldn't be in my position unless I had the instruments, could I?

John Then where . . . ?

Paul Ah.

John In the desk? There's a special drawer in the − ?

Paul No. Stuffed to the brim with directives. The girl. The girl has the instruments.

John The girl?

Paul Gita. Did you see Gita on your way in?

John No.

Paul Well yes, easily missed, Gita. Can't speak. Can't hear. It's a condition. But we found her a place. Inclusion.

John Tell her to bring the instruments in.

Paul She may be −

John Tell her to bring the instrument or I won't talk.

Paul *goes to a door, opens it, beckons.*

Enter **Gita**.

Paul   You're looking very good today, Gita. We're almost ready. We've almost finished talking and we're almost ready for the instruments. Could you get them ready, Gita? Thank you.

Exit **Gita**.

Paul   She's very good. Back in a minute. So – tell me. Tell me why you're so different.

John   Am I?

Paul   Oh yes. Totally different. I've never seen . . . Normally I see fear, anger. Sometimes . . . sullen, nothing. But you're keen. Because . . . ?

John   Because. Because I want to be free. Free of, of, of me. Of all this. I want it to be Cut away. I want to be Cut away from this body. Yes – and this history and this wanting and this busyness and this schooling and these, these ties. I want to be released.

Paul   And you think – ? You really think?

John   Yes, yes.

Paul   You think that's what the Cut – ?

John   I know. I know that's what the Cut does.

Paul   You're very idealistic.

John   I don't think so.

Paul   Bit of a dreamer.

John   No.

Paul   Yes, dreamer. Because, look . . . wouldn't we all? Wouldn't we all like – ?

John   We can.

Paul   We'd all like to be free. Believe me, I want to be free of bodies, of history, of wanting . . . I'd like that just as much as . . .

John   Then . . . free yourself.

Paul   I can't.

John   You can. Anybody can.

Paul   No. No. I Cut. You are Cut. That's my burden.
Nobody's ever changed that –

John   But if you –

Paul   We can stop Cutting. But we'll still be the people who
used to Cut. You'll still be the people who used to be Cut.
Always the same. No fucking point. We soften the blow. Maybe
we end the Cut. But still the old circles, the old divides. Young
and I thought – change it all. I can make it all better. Nothing's
going to be the same. Out with the last lot. And now look at
me. Repellent. Can't tell my beautiful wife, my beautiful
children –

John   Listen, listen, listen.

Paul   What does it matter? Send my beautiful children to the
prison or the university, still they'll be . . .

John   Listen to me.

Paul   They'll always be Cutters, never Cut.

John   I want to show you.

Paul   The old lot, the new lot. Everything's the same. We've
changed nothing.

John   Ssssh. Ssssh. I've got something to show you.

Paul   Yes?

John   Yes. I've discovered . . . I want to share . . . I always
knew what the Cut was going to be, okay?

Paul   Alright.

John   Liberty. Freedom. Nothingness. I knew that. Don't ask
me how. But from dot I knew, so I . . .

Paul   Yes?

John   Prepared myself. Practised little moments of emptiness. Not for ever like the Cut but moments. And you can do that.

Paul   I can't.

John   You can. Each of us can. Each and every one of us can free ourselves.

Paul   Not me.

John   If only you'll . . . shut your eyes.

Paul   No.

John   Please.

Paul   No. I'm sorry. But you understand. After the incident. With the gun. After the incident with the gun I find trust impossible.

John   Of course.

Paul   Which has made lovemaking with my wife, which has made it – does this embarrass you?

John   No, no.

Paul   Which has made lovemaking with my wife impossible. It's only when you can't . . . when you can no longer close your eyes during the, the, the . . . act that you realise . . . lovemaking with the eyes wide open . . . impossible.

John   I see.

Paul   Unnerving for her, embarrassing for me.

John   Of course. I've been searched.

Paul   But if you strangled me.

John   Beat me away. Beat me to the ground. Beat me to death. I'm weak. You're strong. You can easily beat me.

Paul   Yes, yes, I suppose I can.

John   But I'm not going to strangle you.

Paul   No?

John   No. Now please. The eyes.

Paul *closes his eyes.*

Long silence.

John   And there's total darkness.

Paul   Well, almost.

John   Please don't speak. That's vital. It's vital that you don't speak.

Paul   I understand.

John   Ah-hah. Total darkness. And you have no body. Your body has dissolved. Dissolved or melted away. Every piece of skin or bone or hair. Every last cell gone away. The cage has vanished. And you are free.

Feel the darkness. Feel the void.

Remember how they used to scare you with that? Remember then how you used to scare yourself with that?

The darkness. Where the monsters live. Where the witches live. Where the paedophiles are. The darkness. Don't go into the darkness. Carry the candle. Leave a light in the window. Take a torch into the woods.

Lies. All of it lies.

The void. It'll eat you up. The chasm that swallows the sailors, swallows the ships, swallows the astronauts. The hole, the pit, the gap. Avoid. Avoid. Avoid. Take a map, make a rope bridge. Steer clear of the void.

Lies lies, all of it lies.

They've told you lies and you've kept your eyes open. When all freedom asked of you was to close your eyes.

And now you've closed them. And you've made a start.

But still you're trying to work out where the light switch is. Still the torch is in your hand. Still you're fingering the switch. In case. In case. In case.

Don't. Please. I beg you. Spin around. Spin around until
you're dizzy and there's no light switch. Let the torch fall from
your hand. Let it roll away into the forest. Let the mud suck it
up and rot it away.

And stand in the darkness. And become the darkness.

The truth.

And feel everything go.

There's no history. All that struggling to move forward, to
expand, to progress. That's gone away.

And there's no society. All the prisons and the universities have
fallen down or been exploded. Or maybe they never were. It
doesn't matter.

The truth.

And your wife and your children. Eaten away by cancers or
burnt to nothing or maybe never born. Generation after
generation never born. Back and back until the first stroke
of the first day of the first time. None of it ever was.

The truth.

And so there's nothing.

Don't fight. Don't try and feel your body. Don't reach for the
reports. Don't try and call your wife.

Because it's all nothing.

There's only truth. There's only you.

Darkness is light. Void is everything. You are truth.

Long silence.

And open your eyes.

And open your eyes.

And open your eyes.

Paul   I don't want to.

John Open them.

Paul No.

John I've got a gun. In my hand. Pointing at you. I'm squeezing the trigger.

Paul *opens his eyes.*

John Sorry. I had to –

Paul No gun? No gun? Where's the fucking gun? You said there was a –

John Yes, because you wouldn't –

Paul Listen, son, don't fuck around. If there's a gun then have a fucking gun, okay? Okay? Okay?

John I was just trying –

Paul Fuck. I wanted to . . . I didn't want to open my . . . why did you make . . . ?

John Because it's not healthy.

Paul Healthy? Healthy? Healthy? Fuck you. Fuck you. Fuck you. Sorry. Sorry. Sorry.

Pause.

I'm sorry. I really wanted . . . I just wanted you to shoot . . .

John It was a tactic.

Paul Really thought you'd shoot me. That's what I wanted. I wanted to be shot with my eyes shut.

John I wouldn't do that.

Paul But then – cunt that I am – I opened my eyes. Fucked up. Because I'm – what? – a coward. And you – cunt – no gun. We're both cunts. Everyone's cunts. Everything's a cunt. The whole shebang is one big fucking cunting cunty cunt.

John No, no.

Paul Because that's what you're . . . preaching, isn't it? In your . . . sermon.

John   I don't use words like that.

Paul   But you are. That's what you're saying. Everything's shit. Everything's fucked up. There's nothing worth crap.

John   No, no.

Paul   We've tried everything and it's all a void. That's what you said.

John   No I didn't. No I didn't.

Paul   Yes you did. Please don't correct me. I know. I know. What were you doing? Talking. Blah. Blah. Blah. But I, I was listening. With my eyes shut. And I know what I heard.

John   From your perspective.

Paul   The truth. Everything's finished. Everything's over. We're all done.

John   You're twisting everything –

Paul   Listen son. I'm old. I'm wise. You gibber. I shift the shit and pick out the gems. Okay? Okay? Okay?

John   Okay.

Paul   And you're right. And I admire you. I revere you. To say what's been in my head, what I've never been able to . . . the articulation. Because, as you said, I was afraid and I have been lied to. For generations.

And there in the dark. In the moment. I saw. I'm worthless.

I'm a piece of shit. I'm a speck of shit on a lump of shit on a piece of shit. I'm nothing.

And I don't want to carry on.

And I do have . . .

He produces a gun.

Shoot me.

John   No.

Paul As an act of kindness.

John No. I'm not an emotional –

Paul Yes, yes, yes. Go. Off you go.

John No.

Paul It's going to get very bloody in here. I'm going for the head. Blood and brains all over the place. And I don't want you to be a part of that.

John You mustn't.

Paul Here. I'll stamp your report. Show it to the girl on the desk. She'll give you your travel money home. We pay reasonable second class fares. Go back to your village – I take it you have a village and a – and a family.

John No.

Paul Alright. You might want to stand back. Blood in your hair and so on.

John Don't be so . . . don't be so . . . no, no, no. I'm here. I'm here for the Cut. That's what I'm here for. That's what you're supposed to do. You're supposed to administer the Cut.

Paul I'm supposed to . . .

John That's your duty. That's your calling. That's why you were chosen.

Paul Yes, well, I'm . . .

John And that's why I'm here. That's what I've waited so long for. This is what I've been planning for.

Paul I'm sorry. Things change.

John No, no, no. The clips, the books, waiting, waiting, planning, planning. Every moment I ever lived for this moment, you can't oh please oh please oh please oh please oh please . . .

Paul There's a tear.

John Yes.

Paul   You've got a tear.

John   Yes.

Paul   That's very emotional . . .

John   I know. Sorry. Sorry. Where's Gita? Where are the instruments?

Paul   They're being sterilised.

John   Please. Bring them in.

Paul   We have to reuse them. Public finances. But also sterilise them. Public health.

John   I understand. Please. Show me the instruments.

Paul   You're a very selfish young man.

John   Yes.

Paul   To ride roughshod over my suffering.

John   I know, I know.

Paul   Have you any idea of the burden for a man – of my class?

John   No.

Paul   No, no, you don't. Very well.

He rings a bell.

John   Thank you.

Paul   This evening I shall drive my wife to the university. She's made a fruit cake. Our son is reading Advanced Politics. But he still enjoys his fruit cake. And I shall watch her handing over the fruit cake. But all the time I'll be suffering. Like nobody can believe. And I'll wake up tomorrow. And I'll say: today I'll shoot myself. That kid who got the Cut was right. I should shoot myself.

John   Are the instruments . . . ?

Paul   Coming. The kid was right. I should shoot myself. But I won't. Oh, I'll look at the gun. I'll handle it. All day long under the desk I'll be handling the gun. But I won't fire. I won't fire tomorrow or the next day or the next day or the next day or the next day. Or never. I'll be permanently not shooting myself. Can you imagine the horror of that? No you can't. Of course you can't. You – you – you . . . shit.

Enter **Gita**, *carrying the instruments.*

Paul   Ah, Gita, thank you, thank you. Gita's just joined us. She's still training but she's doing very well. Down there, Gita.

Gita *places the instruments down and steps back.*

John   Can I touch them?

Paul   Well, it's not a regular . . .

John   Please.

Paul   Of course. No, no, Gita. It's alright. Stay.

John *picks up the instruments.*

John   These are . . . twenty-three years old.

Paul   Public finances. Lack of investment.

John   From a workshop in the north. The northwestern workshop.

Paul   Very impressive.

John   Look at them. Just look.

Paul   I'm afraid they're purely functional to me.

John   No, no, no. Classic craftsmanship. This is an honour. Thank you. Thank you.

Paul   Shall we get on with it?

John   Yes.

Paul   Gita.

Gita *comes forward.*

Paul   I envy you. I envy everything about you. If you could give me a word. Just a word so I can shoot myself.

John No.

Paul You've broken me.

John I didn't mean to.

Paul That doesn't make it any fucking better. Gita. The lights.

Gita *switches off the lights. Total darkness.*

Paul You are here for the Cut. Please prepare yourself for the Cut.

Long, long pause.

Paul I don't want to . . .

John You have to.

Paul Please, I can't . . .

John Now. Do it now.

Paul Fuck it. Fuck it. Fuck it. The Cut is about to take place.

Long, long pause. **John** *gasps as the instruments go in.*

John Thank you. Thank you. Thank you.

Scene Two

Paul's *flat*. **Paul** *and* **Susan**.

Susan   She's like a child. Quite honestly like a simple little child. I walk in and she's looking at it boiling over. Actually standing there and watching – just . . . watching as it's boiling over. And I say, 'Mina – the milk's boiling over,' and she says, 'Yes, Miss,' and then she carries on, carries on looking.

Paul   Mmm.

Susan   And I suppose I should have been angry. I suppose angry would have been an altogether appropriate response. Would you have been angry?

Paul   Well . . .

Susan   I think you might have been. I think you might have flown into one of your rages.

Paul   Well . . .

Susan   Oh yes, I can see you now tearing into her. Just tearing straight into her.

Paul   I don't know.

Susan   But somehow I . . . I . . . I smiled, maybe – I think I laughed a bit, I indulged . . . yes, alright, I indulged . . . and I said, 'Maybe if you turned down the . . . you see?'

Paul   Mmmmmmm . . .

Susan   And she did. She did when I actually told her what to do.

Paul   Well good.

Susan   But of course tomorrow we'll be right back to square one. She'll be watching it boil over all over again. Little goldfish.

Paul   Yes.

Susan   It's a great pressure on me. This watching. All the time watching, guiding. There's a burden.

Paul   Of course.

Susan   Sometimes half an hour with her . . . I have to lie down. In the dark. For several hours.

Paul   We could have her reassigned.

Susan   I went to the hospital.

Paul   Shall I look into having her reassigned?

Susan   I went to the hospital. But really I was fobbed off. A few tablets. They're useless.

Paul   Let's get her reassigned.

Susan   And can you imagine the fuss?

Paul   There needn't be a fuss.

Susan   You haven't seen the family. You're never here when the . . . Oh, there's a father. And a mother. And a brother. I suspect that she has a child.

Paul   Really?

Susan   I suspect. Just a . . . And they'll all be round here crying and pleading and looking and . . .

Paul   Really? Really? Really?

Susan   You don't know. You just don't know. Oh yes. I don't think I can handle the fuss.

Paul   So we'll keep her?

Susan   I don't know. I don't know. I suppose. I suppose we must. I suppose I'll just have to do the best I can.

Paul   You're a remarkable person.

Susan   Thank you.

Paul   No. I mean it. You're a remarkable person. And I appreciate what you do. For us.

Susan   Supper will be late.

Paul   I just want you to know . . . you're valued.

Susan   After the milk and everything . . . there'll be a wait for supper.

Paul   Ah well.

Susan   So just try . . . try not to get angry until the food arrives.

Paul   I'm not going to . . .

Susan   I know you, I know you. Your blood sugar . . . if the blood sugar's not even that's when you start to get . . .

Paul   What? What?

Susan   You get tetchy.

Paul   No, no, no.

Susan   It's always the same. Yes, yes, yes. You're always the same. So just hold on.

Paul   You know me.

Susan   Oh yes.

Paul   You know me very well.

Susan   I know you totally.

Paul   Ah.

Susan   I know you absolutely and totally.

Paul   Yes. Yes. Is that boring?

Susan   Darling . . .

Paul   A man with no secrets?

Susan   Darling.

Paul   Is it dull to have no doors left to open?

Susan   It's . . . comfortable. I'd say we're comfortable. Wouldn't you say we're comfortable?

Paul   Yes.

Susan   Yes. Comfortable's the word.

Paul   But physically . . .

Susan   You know there's a big push now. From the universities. I got a letter from Stephen.

Paul   Mmm?

Susan   Today. Stephen wrote from the university. He's looking forward to his fruit cake. Stephen wrote and he said there's a big push now in the universities. The students mainly. But also the lecturers. And there's a big push against the Cut.

Paul   Really?

Susan   Yes. That's what he said.

Paul   Really?

Susan   Yes. There's a real groundswell of . . . there's a real mood for ending the whole thing.

Paul   Really?

Susan   What do you think?

Paul   If that's what Stephen −

Susan   Yes. But what do you think?

Paul   I think, I think −

Susan   I think they're right. I think they're absolutely . . .

Paul   Really? Really?

Susan   I think these reforms, these, these, these new criteria . . . I mean softening the blow I think that's . . . I think that's . . . dressing . . . and I think it's time . . .

Paul   What's he doing?

Susan   Mmm?

Paul   What's Stephen . . . ?

Susan   I don't . . . writing . . . stuff . . . they have papers and . . . discussions and . . . I don't . . .

Paul   So . . . talking?

Susan   Talking and writing. Yes. Yes.

Paul   Ah, ah, ah, ah. Student stuff.

Susan   It's a start.

Paul   Is it? Is it? Is it?

Susan   Shall I hurry her along?

Paul   What?

Susan   Mina. Shall I hurry her along?

Paul   Why?

Susan   You're getting tetchy. It's starting.

Paul   No.

Susan   I can see it. The blood sugar's . . . dropping. There's a . . . you're starting to snap.

Paul   No. No. It's just . . . politics.

Susan   Yes?

Paul   It makes me uncomfortable.

Susan   I'm sorry.

Paul   No. No. But I've . . . I've had a day.

Susan   Of course.

Paul   I've had a day and all I wanted was to get back to you and sit with you and eat and read and . . .

Susan   Talk.

Paul   And talk, yes, of course talk and so of course I find it uncomfortable . . .

Susan   Of course. What did you do?

Paul   Mmm?

Susan   What did you do today?

Paul   Oh. Nothing.

Susan   You always say . . . Really? Really? Nothing?

Paul   Well nothing of . . . numbers, figures, reports, dossiers.

Susan   Ah.

Paul   I've got a title. I've got an office. I've got a big office. But really, really I'm just a rubber stamp.

Susan   No, darling.

Paul   Yes, really.

Susan   No, darling. I'm sure . . . I know you're much much much more than a rubber stamp.

Paul   No.

Susan   I try to imagine what you do. I try to picture it. I lie on my bed in the dark in the afternoon. And Mina is breaking something. She's always breaking something in the next room. And I try to block her out. It's better now I've got the pills. And I block her out and I try to picture what you're doing.

Paul   Really?

Susan   Really. I actually try to get a picture in my head of what you're up to.

Paul   And what do you see?

Susan   Ah, ah, ah.

Paul   Come on. What do you see?

Susan   Well, darling . . .

Paul   It's a pretty stupid thing to do, isn't it?

Susan   Is it?

Paul   I should say so. Pretty stupid pointless fucking thing to do. Lying on the bed in the middle of the afternoon. What the fuck are you doing lying on the bed in the afternoon? You shouldn't be lying on the bed in the afternoon. What's wrong with you? There's nothing wrong with you. If there's anything wrong with you we'll find you a better fucking hospital. A better fucking hospital and find some pills that really do the trick.

Susan   Hey, hey, hey.

Paul   But there's nothing wrong with you. There's nothing wrong. You think the world's such a bad place? You talk to Stephen and you think that the world is such a bad place, then fucking do something about it.

Susan (*going to door*)   Mina. Mina.

Paul   Writing. Discussions. Just fucking do something. For the losers. Take them some clothes. Go through the wardrobe and take them some clothes. Or take them some food. Bake a fucking fruit cake. Bake a hundred fucking fruit cakes and go out to the villages and give out the fruit cake. And help instead of lying on the fucking bed in the afternoon.

Susan   Mina. I'm calling you.

Paul   I'm talking to you.

Susan   No you're not.

Paul   Why is your life so petty? Why is your existence so utterly meaningless?

Susan   I'll talk to Mina and we'll get the food on the table.

Paul   So meaningless that you have to imagine me at a desk in the afternoon.

Susan   Hold your horses. The food's on its way.

Paul   I don't want the fucking food.

Susan   Yes you do. Yes you do. Your blood sugar –

Paul   Fuck's sake.

Susan   – has now swung into the danger zone.

Paul   Blood sugar in the danger zone? Where do you get this, where does this – ?

Susan   You're always like this. The danger zone spells tetchiness.

Paul   What is this? Some clip you've seen?

Susan   We need to treat this as soon as we possibly can.

Paul   I'm not your patient. I'm not here for −

Susan   Let's feed you, darling. Let's feed you and everything will be alright.

Enter **Mina**.

Susan   Mina. Mina. Where is the food? The food is very late. We've been waiting. And it's not you that suffers. It's never you that suffers. Mister is suffering because of his blood sugar −

Paul   Agh.

Susan   And Miss is suffering because Mister is suffering and Mister is now tetchy. Bread straight away. Supper as soon as you can.

Exit **Mina**.

Susan   Like a child. Look at her. Never really understands.

Paul   Will we fuck tonight?

Susan   I don't know.

Paul   Really? Really? You don't know?

Susan   How should I know?

Paul   Maybe because . . .

Susan   It's not something we can plan for.

Paul   No.

Susan   I would really rather that was spontaneous.

Paul   Well, let's see, we haven't . . .

Susan   I'd rather that was something that just happened between us.

Paul   It's been six months.

Susan   Has it?

Paul   Give or take − yes, six months.

Susan   Because, because . . .

Paul   So I should say . . . six months. At least. More like seven or eight . . .

Susan   No.

Paul   Eight months. I should say the chances of a fuck tonight are pretty slim.

Susan   Well maybe, yes, maybe.

Paul   I would say definitely.

Susan   Alright then.

Paul   I would say definitely zero.

Susan   Alright.

Paul   Why is that do you think?

Susan   Well, because . . .

Paul   Why is there nothing spontaneous happening between us?

Susan   I should say because . . . because . . .

Paul   Why do you sleep in Stephen's old room, wait till you think I'm asleep then pad along the corridor to Stephen's room?

Susan   Because . . .

Paul   Why have I been tossing myself to sleep for eight fucking months?

Susan   Because you always kept your eyes closed.

Paul   Did I?

Susan   Yes. Because your eyes were shut. Not just . . . squeezed tight. From start to finish.

Paul   Crap. Crap.

Susan   True. True. Fucking true and you know it. And you wept.

Paul   What?

Susan   Eyes squeezed tight with great tears down your cheeks.

Paul   This is . . .

Susan   Your chest holding in the . . . some grief. Grieving as we fucked.

Paul   No, no, no.

Susan   Please don't . . . Grieving as we fucked. And eventually . . . as a woman . . . you don't . . . you can't . . .

Paul   Why do you have to spout this shit? Why do you let this crap come out of your mouth?

Susan   I know. I saw.

Paul   Have you ever seen me cry? Do I look like a man who cries? Has there ever been a day . . . ? Christ, we've known each other for fucking generations. Under the last lot. Under the new lot. We've been together for so fucking long. And have I ever been a crying man?

Susan   Only when we –

Paul   So please don't give me this . . . because I really don't need this, this, this, this shit.

Susan   How can you just, just – ?

Paul   SHUT UP. SHUT THE FUCK UP.

Silence. Enter **Mina** *with bread on a plate.*

Susan   Thank you Mina. Did you get this from the – ? Well, you better get back to the . . . Mina, there's a chip on this plate. Do you know anything about this chip on the side of this plate here? Listen, you'd better get back to the supper.

Exit **Mina***.*

Susan   Look at this. A chip on the side of the plate here. This was a new set this week. Pristine. She worked her way through the last lot. Boom. Crash. Clump. Sometimes I laugh

at her. And sometimes I just block it all out. What can you do
with a child? Here – it's good bread. I got it myself from the
market. Mina never gets exactly what I want. So I've started to
do the shopping myself. As of this month. And actually, you
know, it's not such a hassle. Actually sometimes it can be quite
good fun bargaining. I think I'll carry on. You need to eat.

Paul *takes a piece of bread and breaks bits off and eats them.*

Susan   It's amazing how quickly the blood sugar level goes
back to normal. Just a bit of bread. One of those little miracles.
Would you like to read Stephen's letter? He wrote to me. But
I'm sure he wouldn't mind – I think he'd be happy if you read it.

Paul   I love you.

Susan   I put the letter down somewhere.

Paul   I love you.

Susan   I was reading it – I was here . . . and then I got
distracted by Mina and I went to the . . . letter in my hand.

Paul   I love you.

Susan   And then I was on the bed in the dark.

Paul   I love you.

Susan   And then back in . . .

Paul   I love you.

Susan   So it must be – unless she's moved it of course, which
is entirely possible . . .

Paul   I love you.

Susan   No. No. Here. Here.

Paul   What?

Susan   Stephen's letter. Do you want to read it?

Paul   Thank you.

He takes the letter.

He's always liked fruit cake.

Susan   Always.

Paul   Can you remember a time when he didn't like fruit cake?

Susan   No. No. I can't.

Paul   Maybe that's why he's always been so happy. Blood sugar's up, eh?

Susan   Yes, maybe that's it.

Paul   I think he's wasting his time.

Susan   Mmm?

Paul   Writing. Discussing. They never change anything.

Susan   Not immediately.

Paul   And then you . . . they actually want it, you know?

Susan   They?

Paul   They want to be Cut.

Susan   Hardly.

Paul   Oh yes, you listen to them. On the bus or . . . they actually want it.

Susan   They can't do.

Paul   You realise the tradition, the . . . it actually means something. It gives them meaning.

Susan   No. No.

Paul   That's the reality of the situation.

Susan   How do you know?

Paul   I overhear, I observe.

Susan   How can you say that?

Paul   Because I am actually out there, day after day. I actually –

Susan   And I'm . . . I go shopping. I go outside too.

Paul Yes?

Susan And I don't overhear . . . So you actually want this to go on? You don't want anything to change? You want this practice, this, well, frankly barbaric . . . you just want this to go on and on and on?

Paul I'm tired.

Susan Are you actually defending – ?

Paul I'd love to talk to you. I'd love to debate with you. That would be a great pleasure. But actually after a day of work –

Susan As I see it – Stephen says . . . you've actually got to be for it or against it.

Paul Grow up.

Susan That's what Stephen says.

Paul Fuck's sake – Stephen is a child. Stephen is a student.

Susan And I think I actually agree with him.

Paul But you – you're a grown, you're a mature, you're an old, older woman, person, I think it's a bit late to be seeing the world in –

Susan I think I may join a group.

Paul – black and white. Goodies and baddies. Us and them. We Cut. They are Cut. Fucking simplistic fucking –

Susan Or I may start, yes, actually I may start a group.

Paul Life isn't simple. Things aren't simple. Don't simplify – let Stephen – fine, he's a student – maybe at the university but don't simplify –

Susan You know what I saw this afternoon?

Paul That's all I'm saying.

Susan I lay on the bed this afternoon. In the dark. I took three pills. You're only supposed to take two but I felt . . . I knew those plates were vulnerable and I was feeling . . .

anyway, I took three tablets and I lay back on the bed, I lay back in the darkness and I tried to picture you . . .

Paul   Listen . . .

Susan   Which I've been doing quite a lot recently. The last – oooh – six months. Lie on the bed in the afternoon and I try to picture what you're doing at your office.

Paul   Don't.

Susan   And often I get no picture at all. Often, actually, my mind's still here. And I'm anxious for the crockery and the ornaments and the windows with Mina on the loose. No pictures at all or sometimes a picture, very dull. You're filing. Writing down some numbers. Few seconds of a very dull picture. That's all it's been before.

Paul   Yes.

Susan   But today. But today. A very clear picture. Suddenly. And you're Cutting. There's a young man. And there's the instruments. And you're Cutting him.

Paul   Yes.

Susan   In your dull little office you were doing the Cut. And I wonder why did that come into my head?

Paul   Why do you think?

Susan   I don't know. It was so clear.

Paul   Were you awake?

Susan   Oh yes. I was looking at the ceiling. Because I noticed a mark. Maybe it was Stephen's letter? Do you think that put the idea into my head?

Paul   That's possible.

Susan   That's the only thing that I can think of. Can you think of anything else?

Paul   The bread's all finished.

Susan   There's more. Mina will bring it.

Paul   I think I've had enough. I find sometimes . . . I get bloated.

Susan   You never said.

Paul   Oh yes. More than a couple of slices I find I have a tendency to get bloated.

Susan   You never told me that before.

Paul   It's a tiny, it's a small thing . . .

Susan   Maybe if we tried another . . .

Paul   It's only really started . . . in the last six months or so.

Susan   I see. I see. These things are sent to try us, aren't they?

Paul   I suppose that's right. Yes. These things are sent to try us. I thought of you this afternoon.

Susan   Really?

Paul   Physically. I thought about you physically this afternoon.

Susan   We'll try another kind of bread.

Paul   And I resolved . . . I'd like us to try again . . . physically. I'd like us to have another go.

Susan   Oh.

Paul   I'd like us to pick up where we left off. Lovemaking.

Susan   That's what you did in your office? Thought about us lovemaking?

Paul   Yes, yes, I did.

Susan   That was rather naughty.

Paul   Yes, yes, it was.

Susan   And I was here. Lying in the bed. Seeing you do the Cut.

Paul   Well.

Susan   Well.

Enter **Mina** *carrying a tray with two main courses and cutlery.*

Susan   Thank you, Mina. Better late than . . . there's a good girl. On the table.

Mina *lays the table.*

Susan   That's it, very good. Do you have a little girl or a little boy, Mina? Which is it? Boy or a girl? I tease her about it all day long. Don't I, Mina? Boy or girl, Mina? Boy or a girl? But she won't tell. You keep your secrets, don't you, Mina? You keep your cards close to your chest. But you've got a little kiddy tucked away at home. I know you do. I've got an instinct. There are no secrets from me, are there? I reckon a boy. We've got two boys. Do you want your boy to have the Cut, Mina? Like his ancestors. Course you don't. Makes you scared. Makes you angry. The Cut. Doesn't it, Mina? Well, don't you worry, Mina. Because that's all going to end. That's all going to change. My son's working on that. I'm working on that. We're going to get rid of the Cut. We're going to hunt them down and chuck them out. They'll be none of them left. There'll be none of them doing the Cut by the time your boy's a man. You'll see. You'll see. Yes. You've done very well. You've done beautifully. Oh, Mina – tomorrow, remind me when I go shopping – we're going to try a new type of bread. Mister is getting bloated so we're going to change the bread. Thank you. You go home. There's a kid waiting for you. Boy or girl, Mina? Boy or girl?

Exit **Mina**.

Susan *sits at the table.*

Susan   Well, this looks pretty good. Once she gets the job done, you know, she actually does it rather well. It's just getting her there that's the challenge. I bet you're hungry. Let's start, darling. Let's start.

Paul   I . . .

Susan   I chose all the ingredients myself.

Paul   I . . .

Susan   Bargained for every last bit of this.

Paul   I . . .

Susan   Meals have tasted better since I did the shopping.

Paul   I, I, I, I, I, I, I . . . (*Cries.*) . . . I, I, I, I, I, I, I . . . (*Cries.*)

Susan   You always feel better after you've eaten.

Paul   I, I, I, I, I, I, I . . . (*Cries/howls.*)

Susan   Darling. Darling. Darling.

Paul   A, a, a, a . . . (*Cries/howls.*)

Susan   You've never been the sort of man who cries. All the time I've known you. The last lot. The new lot. The generations. You've never been the sort that cries. How can I make love to you? How can I make love to a man who cries? Who shuts his eyes and just cries and cries.

Paul   I'm . . . sorry.

Susan   Well, of course you're sorry. We're all sorry. But we still have to eat.

Paul   I don't want this. I don't want . . .

Susan   Look at you. Look at you. Get up. You disgust me. You disgust me when you're like this.

Paul   Why can't I shoot myself?

Susan   That's a self-indulgence. There are children.

Paul   Why do we do this day after day after day?

Susan   I don't know. Because we have to. There are things in this world we just have to do. There are responsibilities.

Paul   Don't you ever cry?

Susan   No, no, no. Not that I remember. Not even this afternoon. Not even when I thought of you . . . no.

Paul   I'm sorry. Sorry. I won't do it again.

Susan   You won't . . . ?

Paul   There'll be no more tears.

Susan   Well, that's good. Shall we eat?

Paul   Yes. Let's eat.

They sit up at the table.

Susan   Tomorrow is fruit cake day. Baking for Stephen tomorrow. What will you be doing tomorrow.?

Paul   Same as always.

Susan   So I shall be very busy. No time for a lie-down tomorrow. No time to think about you.

Paul   That's good.

Susan   Yes, that's good. Isn't it? That's good.

Paul   I love you.

Susan   And then the next day we can drive to the university.

Paul   No. Please listen. Please listen to me. I love you. And I want . . . I wish I could show you all of myself. I wish I could let you into . . . I wish there was no . . .

Susan   Secrets?

Paul   Barriers. I wish there were no barriers.

Susan   Yes. Maybe that would be better.

Paul   But I can't.

Susan   No?

Paul   I want to protect you. I want to protect us. The comfort.

Susan   And is that working? Is . . . this . . . the answer?

Paul   I don't know. Will you stay in the bed with me – all night?

Susan   If that's what you'd like.

Paul   I'd like that very much.

Susan   Alright then. Alright. That's what we'll do.

Paul   I think if we just lie tighter for a night. If we could lie together in the dark and, and, and hold each other then that could be a start.

Susan   Do you have a greasy fork?

Paul   It's a very small thing but I think it would start to make it better.

Susan   Good.

Paul   There is a working party. I heard there was a working party looking into reform.

Susan   Mmm?

Paul   Of the Cut. Within government. There's talk of reform. That's where it will happen. Not with the . . . students. There's a movement within government.

Susan   Well . . . good.

Paul   I think the days are numbered.

Susan   Well don't tell me. Tell Stephen. He's the one to tell. I'm sure he'll be very interested. Will you talk to him on Saturday?

Paul   Of course.

Susan   Well . . . good.

Paul   I'm a good man. At the end of the day I'm a good man.

Susan   Of course you are. Is your fork clean?

Paul   I think so.

Susan   Then please . . . eat.

Scene Three

A room. **Paul** *and* **Stephen**.

Paul   You still look the same.

Stephen   Yes?

Paul   To me. When I look at you, you still look the same. Six months. Sicking up milk on my shoulder. Three years running through the grass. Eighteen. Off to the university. You always looked exactly the same to me.

Stephen   Right.

Paul   And here you are. I look at you. And you still look . . . nothing's changed. To me. Nothing's changed.

Stephen   Dad.

Paul   But maybe you . . . what do you . . . how does it feel to you . . . ?

Stephen   Yeah.

Paul   Does it feel to you, does it feel to you that you've changed?

Stephen   Yes.

Paul   Ah.

Stephen   Yes, it does.

Paul   Ah.

Stephen   I feel as though I've changed.

Paul   Ah.

Stephen   I feel as though, I feel . . . the world has changed. And I have changed.

Paul   Ah.

Stephen   I feel that very strongly.

Paul   Ah, ah, ah, ah. Youth. You're young.

Stephen   Not so –

Paul   But still young. Still young enough. Still young enough not to see . . .

Stephen   Yes?

Paul   It all comes round again. You do the same old stuff again and again and again.

Stephen   No.

Paul   Oh yes. There's only so much shit in the pot and it's swilling around and you're stuck in there long enough you'll spot the same old turds flying your way.

Stephen   No.

Paul   That's the way it is. You listen to me. I'm an old cunt. And old cunts . . . old cunts know this sort of thing.

Stephen   There's been a change.

Paul   Ha!

Stephen   There's been a change. Everything's been turned on its head.

Paul   Black is white. Good is bad.

Stephen   We're starting all over again. All of us together are starting together all over again.

Paul   Very good.

Stephen   There's a chance together to start to build –

Paul   Fantastic. Terrific. I'm proud of you. Good with words. You're good with words. You can outgibber the best. That's good. You were always like that. I can never quite . . . I always . . . suspected words. But you – straight into bed with the little fuckers and start banging away. That's good. Good. Good.

Stephen   This really is a better world.

Paul   You know they turn the light on at five thirty every morning? Every morning that fucking thing goes snap at half past five.

Stephen   I'll have a word.

Paul   Apart from Sundays when − oh, blessed luxury! − it's six o'clock. We're indulged till six on a Sunday.

Stephen   I'll talk to them. See if we can sort something out.

Paul   I don't want favours.

Stephen   I'm listened to.

Paul   I don't need you pulling any favours for me. Don't you do any fucking favours on my account. I'm my own person. You're your own person. You don't want to be accused of, of, of . . . favours.

Stephen   They're, we're not cruel.

Paul   They'll be watching out for that. You've always got to watch out for that. A new lot. Favours being pulled.

Stephen   So you don't want me to try . . . ?

Paul   I don't want you to try anything.

Stephen   Alright. Alright.

Paul   What I want, what I want, what I want, what I want is for you to, to leave well alone.

Stephen   Alright then.

Paul   Just . . . let it be.

Stephen   Okay.

Paul   How's your mother?

Stephen   She's fine.

Paul   Good. Good. Good.

Stephen   Mina lost her baby.

Paul   The light goes off soon.

Stephen   Mina had a baby. Inside her. Mina was pregnant. But then she lost the baby. Mother helped with the funeral. She dug.

Paul   Your mother?

Stephen   Yes. She dug the hole.

Paul   Your mother dug the hole? Your mother dug a hole?
Oh. Ha, ha, ha! I'm sorry. But that is fucking funny. Don't you
think that is fucking funny?

Stephen   I . . .

Paul   No. I'm sorry. Come on. The thought of your mother,
the thought of your mother, the thought of her actually
standing there with a spade and the earth and the . . . that is
fucking funny, isn't it?

Stephen   Is it?

Paul   Well, of course it is. Of course it is. What's . . . can't
you see the humour in . . . ?

Stephen   No.

Paul   Oh come on. Have you lost all . . . ? Laugh, for fuck's
sake. Smile. Just let yourself . . . Fuck. Fuck. Fuck.

Stephen   Everything's changed. Everything's new. And in
the new circumstances . . .

Paul   Yes? Yes?

Stephen   And in the new circumstance it is quite appropriate,
it is fitting, it is right, that my mother, that your wife, should
dig a hole.

Paul   Listen to yourself. Listen to yourself.

Stephen   Dad.

Paul   Dig a hole? You sound comical. You sound . . .
ridiculous. You sound fucking ridiculous.

Stephen   To you maybe.

Paul   So get down off your high . . . stop being so fucking
pompous. And laugh.

Stephen   That's not appropriate.

Paul   At yourself. At her. At me. If you like – come on. Rip the piss out of me. Rip the piss out of this whole shitty shebang.

Stephen   I don't want to.

Paul   Christ's sake, fuck's sake . . . is there no humanity left? Do you none of you have a little fucking speck of humanity?

Stephen   Don't you tell me – don't you tell me –

Paul   Alright.

Stephen   – about humanity. How can you tell me about humanity when you, you . . . ?

Paul   Alright, alright, alright.

Stephen   When you . . . the Cut. It's not me, it's not us . . . we never . . . year after year . . . the instruments . . .

Paul   Yes.

Stephen   Humanity? Humanity? Humanity?

Paul   You're right. Did you never think . . . ?

Stephen   No.

Paul   All the years and you never thought for a . . . ?

Stephen   No.

Paul   I was a good dad.

Stephen   Yes.

Paul   I think your mother always knew.

Stephen   She says not.

Paul   Every day a little dance around each other because I suspected that she suspected.

Stephen   She told the tribunal –

Paul   Sometimes it was actually quite fun.

Stephen   She told the tribunal that there was never the faintest inkling.

Paul   Did she?

Stephen   Yes.

Paul   Did she really?

Stephen   Yes.

Paul   Well, well, well. Well, I suppose she would. Each to their own, I suppose. You've got to save your own bacon when the chips are down, isn't that right?

Stephen   I think she's telling the truth.

Paul   Oh no, no, no.

Stephen   I could see it in her eyes.

Paul   No, no, no, because I spent the years, I had the years with . . . so don't you . . . no. Lying.

Stephen   No.

Paul   So – this is the bright new future. This is the new world. Kids who can't tell the difference between a lie and the truth. Oh son. Oh son, I would weep but there's no more fucking tears.

Stephen   The tribunal cleared Mother.

Paul   Well, that's good.

Stephen   But the house was in your name, so . . .

Paul   Ah . . .

Stephen   They're using it as a prison.

Paul   More prisons? A better world with more prisons?

Stephen   There are certain temporary . . .

Paul   Yes, of course. Of course. Of course. Would you say I'm evil?

Stephen   I . . .

Paul   No. Just look at me now. And would you say I'm evil?

Stephen   I . . .

Paul   No. The heart. The gut. The soul. Listen. Listen. Listen to them now. And would you say . . .

Stephen   Yes.

Paul   . . . that I'm evil?

Stephen   Yes.

Paul   Ah.

Stephen   Yes. There are systems of evil. There are acts of evil. There are people of evil. I say that there are all of these things. Yes. There is evil. And you are evil. You are it. You are my father and you are evil. That's what I say. Yes. Yes. Yes.

Paul   I see.

Stephen   That's not personal . . . please don't take that the wrong . . .

Paul   It's alright.

Stephen   Please. I'm sorry. I'm sorry.

Paul   No. Don't be. I bless you. Come here. Let me hold you.

Stephen   No.

Paul   Please. Let me hold you so I can bless you for that.

Stephen *moves to* **Paul.** **Paul** *holds him.*

Paul   Bless you for that. Bless you for that. Bless you for that.

Stephen *moves away.*

Paul   You're honest. I'll give you that. We were never honest. Me. Your mother. The whole lot of us. We were never honest but you're . . .

Stephen   I try.

Paul   So maybe it's better, yes? Maybe that's a bit better than before?

Stephen   We like to think so.

Paul   Cold but honest. You are the future, my son.

Stephen   And you . . .

Paul   And I'm . . . yeah, well, you're right about me. What
you say. I'm . . . yes, I am. Totally. In act and, and, and, and . . .
soul. Totally.

Stephen   But if you just . . .

Paul   No.

Stephen   There is forgiveness. That's what we . . .

Paul   No.

Stephen   The Ministry of Forgiveness has hearings. You'll
be heard. I can arrange for you to be heard. If you say what
you've just said to me, you acknowledge, you can . . .

Paul   No.

Stephen   There is a way forward.

Paul   I don't want to . . . no. I want punishment.

Stephen   There are no –

Paul   I want to be paraded and scourged and feel the blood
in my eyes and see the blades before me. I want to know that
everyone sees my rottenness and is ready to Cut it out.

Stephen   What? What?

Paul   I am the dirt that needs to be destroyed so you can be
purified.

Stephen   What? Where do you get the . . . ? No. No.

Paul   That's what I want.

Stephen   That's so . . . old-fashioned.

Paul   Yes. Isn't it? Isn't it? Isn't it?

Stephen   That doesn't happen any more.

Paul   I know. I know. So. I'll sit it out. Lights on at five-thirty,
six days a week. Sunday indulgence. Sit it out till there's a new
lot or this lot falls back on some of the old ways.

Stephen   That isn't going to happen.

Paul   It always happens. Sooner or later. Sooner or later when the forgiveness is done there'll be scourging again and I'll be here. I'll be ready for it. It's what I deserve. I'm evil. It's what I deserve. The light's going to go. Any moment now that light's going to go blink and then there's going to be total blackness. So you had better piss off. Go on. Go on.

Stephen   Dad.

Paul   You don't want to get stuck in the darkness. You go. There's a better world out there.

Stephen   Goodbye.

Product

Product was first presented by Mark Ravenhill and Paines
Plough at the Traverse Theatre, Edinburgh, on 17 August 2005.
The cast was as follows:

James   Mark Ravenhill
Olivia   Elizabeth Baker

Director   Lucy Morrison
Lighting and Sound Designer   Mat Ort

Characters

James
Olivia

An office. **James**, *a film producer and* **Olivia**, *an actress.*

James   So there's a knife.

And your eyes widen as you see the knife.

And he's pulled it out from under his . . . the knife comes out from . . . he's wearing a, a . . . robe.

He's a tall fellow, a tall, dusky fellow, and –

And now he uses the knife, he uses the knife and he slits open the plastic on his croissant and he puts the croissant in his mouth and he puts the knife in that sort of stringy pouch in front of him.

Now you want to call out – you are just about to call out:

'He's got a knife. The tall dusky fellow has got a knife.'

But something – a decision, a small but important beat, you don't call out. You look down the aisle at the tanned and blonde and frankly effeminate airline staff and you don't call out.

Why? Why? Why? Well . . .

Let's just discover her, shall we? Let's just discover Amy, a beat at a time.

'Excuse me,' you tells the dusky fellow, 'that's my seat.' You've had the window seat since childhood and he stands to let you in and you open the overhead baggage container – your luggage is Gucci, Gucci are in, it's going to be fabulous, you opens the luggage container and . . .

There's a mat. A small oriental mat rolled up very neat.

Hold on your face. Suprise, apprehension, maybe, I just want you to . . . play it.

'Is this yours?'

'Yes.'

'Do you do yoga?'

'No. That is my prayer mat. I pray.'

'Oh.'

And you sit and you . . . you look out the window and you . . . fear . . . you're in an, an aeroplane up in the air, next to a tall dusky fellow whose prayer mat is up above you and whose knife is in the pouch in front of you.

'Ladies and gentlemen. Could I remind you to switch off all electrical goods?'

And you reaches into your bag and you takes out your mobile and you go to switch off your mobile phone and now we – close up on you – you look down at the mobile and something is triggered inside you, a chord of emotion resonates and we see – ah! Amy is wounded, there's a wound and it's something about the mobile, something about the . . . it's a narrative hook and it's empathy.

I know you're going to love her. I hope you're going to love her. She is three-dimensional. And I'd love to see you play three-dimensional again after those last three, four . . .

And now the fellow turns, he turns, the tall dusky, fellow he turns and suddenly his head is on the shoulder of your suit – it's Versace, Versace are in, it's a Versace suit – his dusky head is on the fabulous shoulder of your fabulous Versace suit and he falls asleep.

And you look at, you look at him . . . You . . . His smell is so different.

And do you know what you want to do? Do you know what you want to do? Well, I'll . . .

You want to . . . you actually want to . . . you want to reach out to the knife . . . reach out to the knife and you want to grab hold of the knife, okay, and pull the knife out of that stringy pouch and you want to feel the weight of the blade in your hand and then you want to thrust it into him, in and out and in and and in and out and in out until there is blood, there is blood shooting from that dusky frame and the blood is shooting over you and you're more blood than face and you want to call out:

'This is for the Towers. This is for civilisation. This is for all of us, you bastard.'

You don't say that. You don't do that. That's an interior monologue. You play that? I want you to play that with your eyes. Can you play that with your . . . ? Well of course you can, of course you can. I love your work.

'This is for all of us you bastard.'

You see? You see? Amy is wounded. She is . . . to each of us the wound, to each the wound is different. It sounds classical but it's me, it's my note to my writers . . . show me the wound . . . and . . . please . . . I will show you Amy's wound if you'll – Yes? Yes? Yes?

It's a thrill to have you in the room.

So Amy doesn't touch the knife, she leaves the knife, the knife is untouched and the plane lands and the dusky fellow puts the knife under his robe and he takes his prayer mat from the baggage container and that should be . . . they should never meet again but . . . this is the world of the heart, this is the screen, the dream, this is movie-land, so, so, so . . .

It's a rainy night, a storm at Heathrow, a broken heel on your Jimmy Choos and the only taxi left and it's his taxi, and suddenly he's saying:

'Please – get in.'

Fear but somehow excitement. The adventure has begun. Into the car of a stranger.

And you climb in with fear and excitement and there's the prayer mat and there's the knife on the seat between him and you, and you:

'Which way are you going?'

'I don't know. Which way you going?'

'I – I – I – '

'You gonna take me home?'

Take him home? Take him home? Are you going to take him
home?

Cut to your face. Cut to the knife. Cut to the prayer mat. Cut
to his – and the lighting favours him now, okay? Something in
the lighting – for the first time he looks handsome.

And you, and you, and you – you play the, her aching sexuality.
Which I know you . . .

Your sexuality aches and he's handsome and you ignore the
prayer mat and the knife and you say to the cabbie,

'The docklands please.'

And he says,

'Docklands love, course love.'

And you exit east from Trafalgar Square.

You live in an abbatoir, it's an old converted abbatoir that is
now a massively cool loft-style apartment and it feels good to
be home and strange and exciting to be letting the dusky fellow
in to your world, but you open the door and you let him in and
he puts down the knife and the prayer mat on your floor and
you offer him wine, but he doesn't drink, but you do drink –

'I'm Amy. I open call centres and call centres, I travel around
and around and around in dwindling circles around this
shrinking globe.'

And you're nervous and you drink the better part of a bottle
and your eye occasionally flicks to the knife and the prayer mat
and now you've drunk the bottle and you are . . .

A man, a tall, dusky man in your apartment.

Your sexuality is so . . . it's aching, it's aching . . . it's inflamed
and you – you suprise yourself – but you want him, you want
him, you want the dusky fellow and you, and you press yourself
upon him.

Mohammed.

But he's frightened. He's a virgin and he knows nothing of this world of aching sexuality and he's frightened.

'Amy, I'm frightened.'

'Mohammed, don't be frightened. Don't be . . . Ssssh. Ssssh. Ssssh.'

And you lead him to the bed and it's very beautiful – and you have a body double, Beata is your body double – and you lead him to the bed and you slip his body from his robes and at last your ache can be, can be, can be . . . filled.

And he is slow and unsure and clumsy at first, but then as you move together, body and heart and . . . as you find the music of your . . . and now you begin to come and come and come and come and come and it's the orgasm of your life.

He sings.

To find yourself, to find yourself, you – Amy – with your wound, to find yourself so at one with this dusky fellow is so . . . strange. We have to . . . we have to see that in your face. Can you play that? Can you . . . ? Of course. I love your work. I love it. I've seen you do those turns on a sixpence. Hate. Love. Click. Power. Subjection. Click. I've seen you do that with a shit script and a cast I wouldn't wish on a mini-series. You're fabulous and this is fab – it's gonna be fabulous once it's been punched up.

But then – time passes in the night – time passes in the night and maybe you fall asleep but you wake, you wake – a jolt – uh – and you reach out – you reach out – you reach out and – you're – like so many times before you're alone in the bed.

Has he – ? Has he gone? Has he taken you and gone?

Your eyes adjust to the darkness. No. He hasn't gone. He hasn't . . . There is the prayer mat and there is the knife just where he left them on your floor, so he hasn't gone he's just, he's . . .

And then you see him. You see his dusky frame. You see the
dusky frame moving about your incredibly cool loft-style
apartment – which was once an abbatoir – and you see him
and he's moving about and he's looking at your white goods
and he's looking at your black goods and your chrome goods
and your beech goods and your plasma and your bluetooth
and your exercise equipment and you know, you know, you
know what he's doing and you throw yourself, you throw your
naked – Beata's naked body from the bed and the words just
come up, they just come up from inside you and you scream:

'Stop judging me. Stop fucking judging. So my life is worthless.
So I'm busy but it means nothing. So all I have around me is
clutter and no value. So I never had a belief. So I'm all alone
and I'll let the first human being inside me who shows me the
slightest – '

'So, so, so, so – '

(We had a theatre writer work on this bit.)

'And you, what about you? Who gives you your orders? The
Imam? The Dictator? Allah? Oh, open your eyes, open your
eyes. What would you like to do to me eh? Given half a
chance. Cover me up? Stone me? But you'd like to.'

That's stopped him. That's stopped him in his tracks and he's
just stopped and he's listening to you.

'How can you, how dare you feel superior to me? I am
freedom, I am progress, I am democracy – and you are fear
and darkness and evil and I hate you.'

His sperm is still dribbling down your leg. That's a private note.
We won't shoot it.

And now you, there are tears, you are, the tears come up and
now – your wound – as if on impulse, a beat, fast beat, you
reach for your mobile and you call up a message, a message
from the past, a message from – the time when the wound
began, when all the hurting began to hurt.

And you – message is on conference and you place it there in
the middle of the floor down by the prayer mat and down by

the knife, and you place your mobile phone down and you stand naked and Mohammed stands naked – like Eve, like Eve – and you listen to:

'Oh my God oh my God oh my God oh my God oh my God . . . ' (It can be punched up.)

'Oh my God Amy, something's got the tower. They've . . . the other tower is on fire.'

'And – Amy, sweetheart, I think they've got us too. I think they hit our tower, sweetheart. We're on fire. Shit. We're on fire. And I'm gonna have to jump baby and I – I just want you to know, Amy, I love you, I love you, I love you with all my – aaaaah.'

And the message ends and Amy falls, falls to the floor and sobs. Which I think you can, I know you can . . .

I get a lot of scripts. It's my job. I get . . . there are hundreds of thousands of stories and they're sitting on my desk and mostly they are, they are, they are . . .

The effluent of the soul.

Nobody understands the basic, the truth, the wound.

He sings.

But this script, this story, I – I have been touched, I have been moved by this. When I – I have lain on the floor in my office and wept when I read this script, you see? You see?

And I want to . . .

There are powers greater than me. There is a Higher Power. I cannot greenlight. And I have been to the Power and I have said: 'This is the one, this is the . . . I want to produce this script, I have wept like a woman at this script and now I must tell this story,' and the Power has said to me: 'Get someone big attached.'

And so I – so I – so I – no bullshit – I thought of you. For Amy. You are my first, you are my only choice for Amy –

Because like her you are . . . I know you hurt, I know . . . it's there, it's up there on the screen, your raw wound for me, us all to see which is why you . . .

You fascinate and you excite me.

So let's . . . make a movie.

The message ends. The message from the past, the message from the Towers, and Amy falls to the floor of her fabulous apartment and she is sobbing and now she, she's calling out:

'Troy's gone. I'll never see Troy again. Troy died in the Towers and I'll never see Troy again.'

And Mohammed comes to you and he puts his arms around you.

'Ssssshhh.'

And for a moment, there's comfort, comfort, but then your POV on the knife and the prayer mat and you say:

'Mohammed, I have to know. I have to know, Mohammed.'

'Sssshhh. Not now Amy.'

'Yes, Mohammed I have to – are you Al Queda?'

'Not now, Amy. Ssssh. Sssssssh. Sssssh.'

And he lies you down on the bed and he holds you and, oh, the comfort of that dusky frame.

Now let's not play Amy with any judgement please, no let's not judge . . . let's just . . . let's just play her as a woman, as a woman who that night as she lay there fell in love, fell in love with a man, a man with a knife and a prayer mat, a woman who that night as she slept, as she slept in Mohammed's dusky arms, forgot, forgot for the first time since the eleventh of the ninth of 2001, forgot the smoke and the confusion and the calls, and the droop and crumble of the Towers, and she forgot the fall of Troy.

And let's – moment by moment, day by day – she is drawn into Mohammed's world, moment by moment, day by day, and other men begin to gather at her apartment, other men with their robes and their knives and their prayer mats – seven, then eight, then nine, then ten men at a time, their mats positioned on the floor, calling to Mecca, talking, planning.

Is this is a cell? Is this – a fundamentalist terrorist threat in the middle of your world?

You should ask, you should challenge, but you're – it's love, you're in – wild, blind, stupid – and the Heart is a bigger organ than the Brain, as we say in this business we call show.

And then one day they are there – Mohammed and the men are there with their knives and their prayer mats in your fabulous loft-style apartment, and you're making their infusion and suddenly the door opens, the door opens and you turn and you see, you see, you see, here, in your apartment, coming across your apartment, he's there in your apartment, in your apartment, Osama is in your apartment.

And he comes towards you and he smiles at you – it's a cruel smile – and he . . .

Bless you.

Why don't you – ? There are knives, there are – Why don't you attack? You could, you should, you –

It's inner conflict you're experiencing, you're playing this inner conflict. Everything is – for the sake of Troy, for revenge you should attack, you should revenge but you don't and you are kissed – you are kissed, a warm breathy kiss on the forehead from Osama.

And now the plan is revealed. Now the work of the cell is made known to you. Now you know that they are all evil men.

Europe is to be torn apart. The Hague. The Reichstag. Tate Modern. Suicide bombing. Each of these men is to be stuffed and strapped with explosives and then at midday tomorrow they will carry off buildings and people and nothing but misery and devastation will follow.

And now they're coming to Mohammed. To Mohammed's task. What will be Mohammed's task?

You want to cry out:

'No, no, no, no, Mohammed. I love you.'

Your mouth is open but the words don't come.

And then you discover, then you learn. Osama turns, he turns and he gives Mohammed his mission: Disneyworld Europe. He must blow up Disneyworld Europe.

And now you step forward and you hear yourself saying, as if another is speaking for you:

'I can't bear for you to do this, Mohammed. I can't bear to lose you. I've already lost Troy. And I won't lose you. I'm a woman and I love this man.'

And then you turn to Osama.

'Let me go with him. Strap me and stuff me with explosives and let me go with him and let me die with my man in the middle of the day, in the middle of the continent, at Disneyworld Europe.'

'No woman can ever – '

'Please, great mullah, please. I am a woman but I love this man and I want to die with this man.'

Minutes go by and we cut to the faces of the jihadists as they wait for the decision of Osama, their mullah. Cut to Mohammed – his eyes are misty. Cut to you – waiting, waiting.

And then Osama breathes and he smiles and he nods:

'Yes.'

You are to die with your man.

And that night you lie in Mohammed's arms, you lie and wait the call that will take you to the EuroStar and on to your mission, you lie in the dark and he says:

'I love you, Amy, I love you with all my heart and I thank Allah for your bravery to join me in suicide.'

'It's just something I have to do, Mohammed.'

'But I fear. When my body is blown apart at the beat of twelve I will go to Paradise. It will be easy to leave this world and go to Paradise. Where will you go?'

'I . . . I . . . I . . . I . . . don't know Mohammed. Where there . . . Can I come to Paradise?'

'No. You are not chosen for Paradise.'

'Oh.'

'These are our last hours together.'

'Then fuck me. Fuck me. Fuck me. Fuck me these last few hours. Fill me every way you can until I hurt and I just can't take you any more. Come, Mohammed, come.'

'A place that only we know.'

And he does and you are hungry, hungry, hungry, but finally you're en-seam-ed bodies topple into slumber and then it comes, the nightmare comes.

You are there, you are in Disneyworld Europe and you are stuffed and strapped with every explosive known to man and you look around – a minute to twelve and you look around – and you see the people and you can't see . . . These are good people, these are good, fat, happy, bright people. Queueing, eating, riding people. These are your people. What are you doing? What are you doing?

Forty seconds until you take them away. Forty seconds until you push your hand through all of us and rip it apart.

How can you do this? Why are you doing this?

'*Avez-vous vu ma mère?*'

You look down at the little girl with the ears and the balloon and she's what – three?

'*Avez-vous vu ma mère? Je veux ma mère. S'il vous plaît – je cherche ma mère.*'

And you want to scream:

'No fucking point sweetheart. No fucking point. She's a dead person. I'm a dead person. You're a dead person. We're all just dead people in the Magic Kingdom of Life.'

But you don't – you take her hand – twenty seconds to go, but you take her hand –

You, you suicide jihadist, you take the hand of the pretty little girl with her mouse ears and balloon and you begin to walk down main street because you think: better she has these last few seconds of comfort in the search for maman than to die alone and in fear and despair.

The time is coming in now, it's coming – ten, nine, eight, seven, six –

The explosives on your body are pulsating and vibrating as if to will themselves to their deathly task –

Five –

'*Mama, mama, où est-tu, mama?*'

Four –

A figure is approaching.

'*Bonjour – Je m'appelle Mickey. Tous est ma amie. Comment t'appelles-tu?*'

'I am Death. I am Death. Run, Mickey. Run, Magic Kingdom. I am Death.'

Three –

'*Bonjour – fille jolie. Quelle ballon joli.*'

'*Où est mama?*'

Two –

'*Je ne sais pas. Moi, je ne suis pas ta mère.*'

One. Tiny beat – maybe it's not gonna, maybe it's not – maybe fate and computer error have saved the world but then –

Boom!

From your back and your chest and your sex the force comes, the explosive comes, and in your last moment of your life that child's head, now ripped from its body, and the blood filling your eyes, that child's head is blown towards you and her voice fills your head as you die:

'*Maman.*'

You wake with a start. It's three in the morning, three in the morning in your fabulous loft-style apartment and you look at Mohammed and suddenly you are filled with disgust.

What is this? What are you doing?

He shouldn't be here with you. He shouldn't be – he should be in an orange jump suit and he should be spat at and kicked and humiliated.

You pig. You dog. You worse than animal. Roll in this shit. Piss your pants. Eat your faeces, cunt.

And you are resolved and you reach for the phone and you phone the Special Forces.

And you report everything – sometimes with tears, sometimes in anger – you tell the whole terrible tale.

And now a van is on its way to take . . . Mohammed and the explosives.

Alone again. Another man who turned out to be not right for you. Every year the hurt grows a little more, until one day it will be so raw you'll never love.

Just one last look, one last look at Mohammed before he goes.

He looks like a boy – who could have thought he would be . . . ? He looks like a boy.

And you move toward him and you sit on the bed and you run your fingers through his dark, dark hair.

'I'm sorry, Mohammed, I'm sorry.'

And you lean forward and you kiss a gentle kiss upon the sleeping lips.

'Bitch.'

His eyes snap open, his hand is up and strikes across the jaw.

'Bitch. Bitch. Bitch.'

'Ahhh!'

'Bitch. You have betrayed us.'

His lithe body jumps from the bed and he kicks you in the stomach, there's no breath in your lungs, there's a gob of blood in your mouth.

'You have betrayed Allah.'

'I won't do it. I won't kill innocent children.'

And you fear for your life. You fear that Mohammed will kill you, dismembered corpse in your apartment, and you remember Mohammed's knife. And something inside you says – get the knife – get the knife – it's lying there and he could use the fucking knife and slit me toe to crown. You rush for the knife, you hold it – and you look up. But he hasn't gone for the knife.

He's got a petrol can in his hand. Where did that come from?

He looks down at you. His eyes lock on to yours. The seconds pass. A lorry passes in the night carrying beef to Dover. (That's a detail.)

And now there is sadness in his eyes and he says:

'I am the weakness. I am the flaw. I was the lust that drove me to woman. I have betrayed jihad.'

And he pours the petrol can over his dusky frame, shaking his hair like a girl in a shower after hockey.

'This world is a place of suffering and unhappiness. Yes?'

'Yes, yes, yes.'

'Please, Allah, admit me to Paradise, please Allah. I failed jihad, but please, Allah.'

And now he moves to the Aga and he picks up the matches and you see what he's going to do.

'Mohammed – don't.'

'But I have failed my mullah, I have failed my cause. Goodbye.'

He strikes the match.

'But Mohammed, I love you, I love you, I love you with all my heart more than Troy, more than the Towers, your strength your mystery your heart. I – Let's run away now, before the security forces . . . Let's begin again, there's a cottage, the countryside – '

'No. I have loved you, Amy. But we are just people.'

'That's all there is. People. Lonely, wounded people and their loving hearts.'

'No. There is Destiny, there is Allah's will, there is the Cause. And all of these are bigger than people. I pity you, my love, in your small world of people. No purpose . . . How do you live with this? My sadness is with you.'

He looks up.

'Oh please, Allah, let your servant come to Paradise.'

And then – woosh – he's alight, the flame racing across his body and his skin and hair and crackling and the smell is almost sweet in your converted abbatoir.

And then you – this feeling deep within and you calls out:

'Oh take me, take me, Mohammed. Take me in those arms. I love you. I don't know you. I'll never know you. I will never believe a thing you believe. But fold me in your burning arms, press your flaming chest against me, scorch me with your groin of fire.

Then, as if in slow motion – fuck it, we are in slow motion – you run toward the burning man.

And now – a life avoiding, avoiding, afraid of death (character notes: your mother's cancer, your best friend's suicide, your father dwindling into Alzheimered oblivion), all your life scared, and your denial of death and now the freedom, the total exhilirating three-dimensional freedom as you call on the Angel of Death to take you and –

'Yes, Mohammed. Yeeeeessss!'

And you're closing in on him, you're reaching him, your hair is starting to crack and sizzle as the flames are inches from you and then, then, then, your arms enfold him and his skin begins to melt onto yours:

'Yeeessssss!'

And then there's the crack of glass – do you know Liz? Fabulous little dyke, gonna be doing all your stunts? – the crack of glass as you both fall and fall and fall, four storeys and into the pool below.

Underwater those bodies, twisting around, the flames becoming smoke, becoming charred and sodden, your bodies twisting one over the other.

Until you come up – eighty-degree burns on his part, twenty degrees for you but –

There's love, like a great wave of release, suddenly there's love, there in the pool there's love and you kiss and caress and you fuck in the water, the pleasure of the lovemaking, the pain of the burns all rolling into one.

And the security forces are on their way, the security forces are . . . But something inside you, you know that Mohammed isn't going to live for . . . there is usually a voice inside – no God, no angels, no nothing in our world but still a voice – that says, you know – he's about to go, the life is about to go and –

Thank you for listening. Thank you for coming here. It's been a privilege to tell the story. And, you know, later if you want to go back to your, you know, manager and agent and PR and your people and, you know, take the piss, use the script to . . . then fine, fine, because at least I've told you, I have told you.

There is actually that moment. We're going to need a fantastic lighting cameraman, but there is actually a moment when the soul leaves the body. Have you ever . . . ? I've seen it. I've seen it and – erm – if we can get that on celluloid then . . . they can fucking kiss my arse.

So Mohammed's soul leaves his body for Paradise.

And you mourn him and you mature in that moment – not in a gradual – bereavement matures you in a moment.

And you look around and you see it's all screens and show and display and symbols and acting make-believe emptiness.

And you pick up the knife and you feel the weight of the knife in your hand and the sharpness of the blade and you turn the blade toward you, oh to do it, to do it, to do it, just to feel the dignity of Ancient Rome.

But then –

Cut to your POV.

And it's the prayer mat.

And you look at the prayer mat. And you play: The knife or the prayer mat? Prayer mat or the knife? Which will it be? Which will you . . . ?

Knife. Prayer mat. Face. Knife. Prayer mat. Face.

And then . . . you put down the knife. You don't kill yourself.

And you move across the floor and you reach the prayer mat and you look around – unsure which way to position yourself – but then –

A sudden swell of certaintity – you're underscored – and then you kneel down, you kneel down upon the mat and – she's a great character:

'Allah? I'm ready, Allah.'

Printed in the USA
CPSIA information can be obtained
at www.ICGtesting.com
LVHW020934171024
794056LV00003B/762